PIANO · VOCAL · GUITAR

LORDE   PURE HEROINE

ISBN 978-1-4803-6698-5

7777 W. BLUEMOUND RD. P.O. BOX 13819 MILWAUKEE, WI 53213

In Australia Contact:
Hal Leonard Australia Pty. Ltd.
4 Lentara Court
Cheltenham, Victoria, 3192 Australia
Email: ausadmin@halleonard.com.au

Visit Hal Leonard Online at
www.halleonard.com

TENNIS COURT

Words and Music by ELLA YELICH-O'CONNOR
and JOEL LITTLE

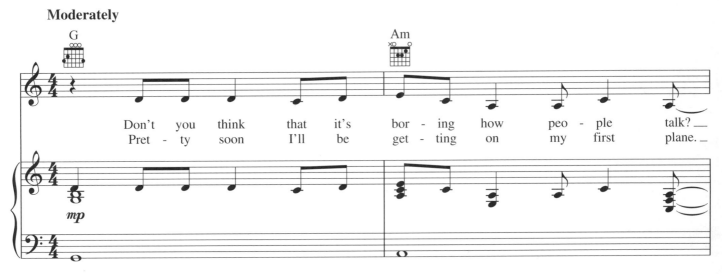

Don't you think that it's bor-ing how peo-ple talk?
Pret-ty soon I'll be get-ting on my first plane.

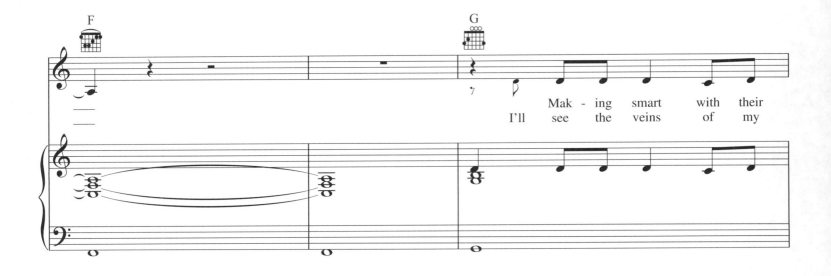

Mak-ing smart with their
I'll see the veins of my

words a-gain, well, I'm bored.
cit-y like they do in space.

Be-cause
But my head's

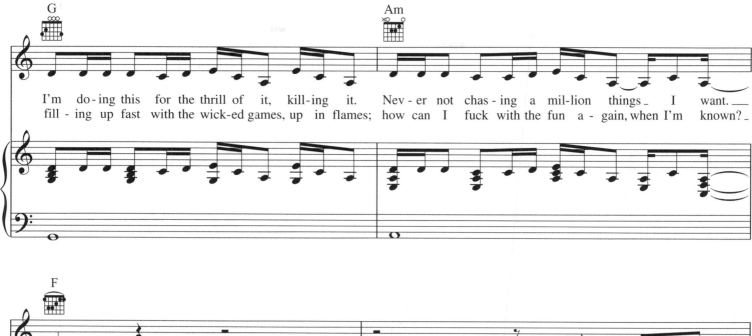

I'm do-ing this for the thrill of it, kill-ing it. Nev-er not chas-ing a mil-lion things_ I want. _
fill-ing up fast with the wick-ed games, up in flames; how can I fuck with the fun a-gain, when I'm known?_

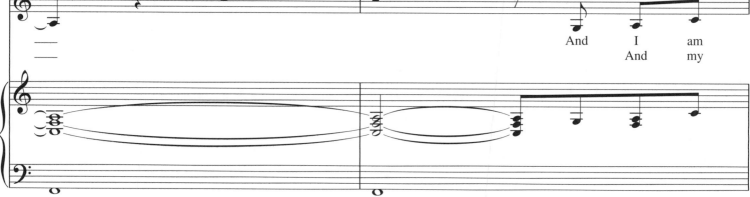

And I am
And my

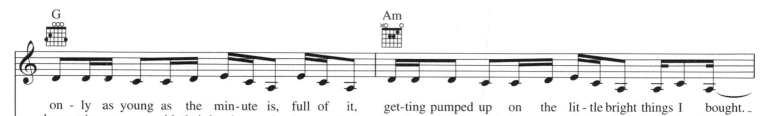

on-ly as young as the min-ute is, full of it, get-ting pumped up on the lit-tle bright things I bought. _
boys trip me up with their heads a-gain, lov-ing them, ev-'ry-thing's cool when we're all in line for the throne. _

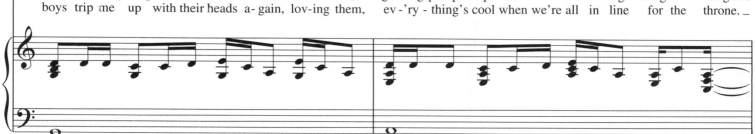

But I know they'll nev-er own me.
But I know it's not for-ev-er.

Ba - by, be the class clown, I - 'll be the beau - ty queen in

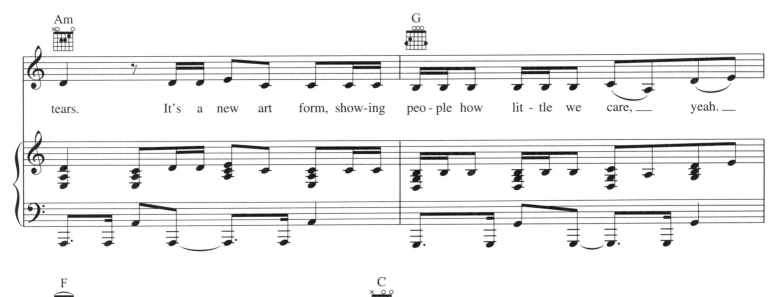

tears. It's a new art form, show-ing peo-ple how lit - tle we care, ___ yeah. ___

We're so hap - py, e - ven when we're smil - ing out of

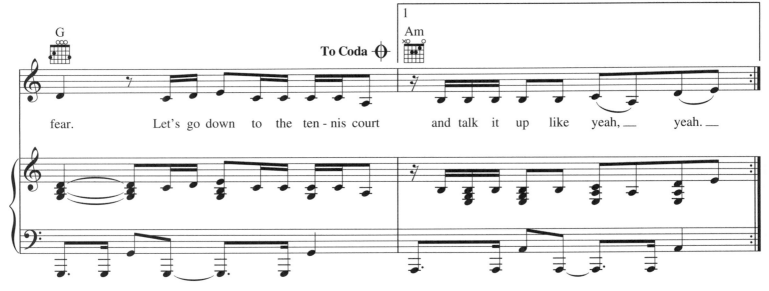

fear. Let's go down to the ten - nis court and talk it up like yeah, ___ yeah. ___

D.S. al Coda

And you could watch from your win-dow.

And you could watch from your win-dow.

CODA

and talk it up like yeah, ___ yeah. ___

And talk it up like yeah, ___ yeah. ___

And talk it up like yeah, ___ yeah. ___

Let's go down to the ten-nis court

and talk it up like yeah, ___ yeah. ___

and talk it up like yeah, ___ yeah. ___

400 LUX

Words and Music by ELLA YELICH-O'CONNOR
and JOEL LITTLE

come a-round here all the time, got a lot to not ____

do, ____ let me kill it with ____ you. You pick me

up and take me home a-gain, __ head out the win-dow a-gain. __ We're

hol-low like the bot-tles that we drain. You drape your

wrists o - ver the steer - ing wheel, _ pul - ses can drive from here. _

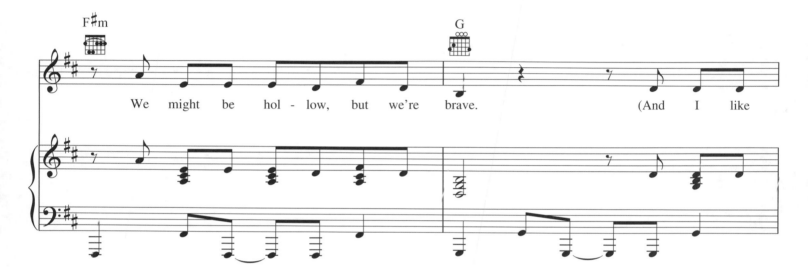

We might be hol - low, but we're brave. (And I like

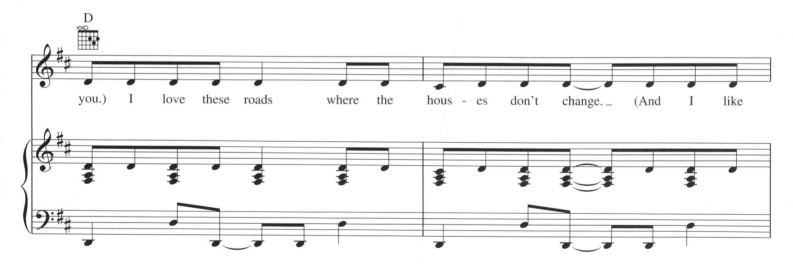

you.) I love these roads where the hous - es don't change. _ (And I like

you.) Where we can talk like there's some - thing to say. ___ (And I like

come a-round here all the time, got a lot to not do,

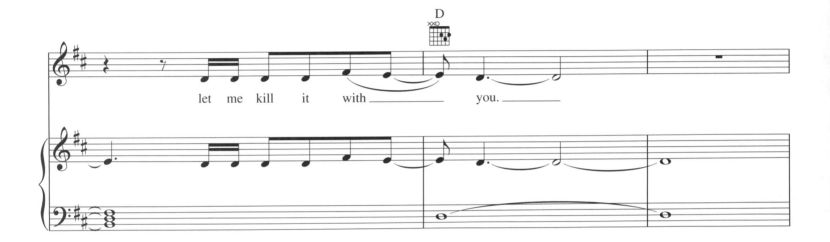

let me kill it with you.

(And I like you.) I love these roads where the

hous-es don't change. (And I like you.) Where we can talk like there's some-thing to say. (And I like

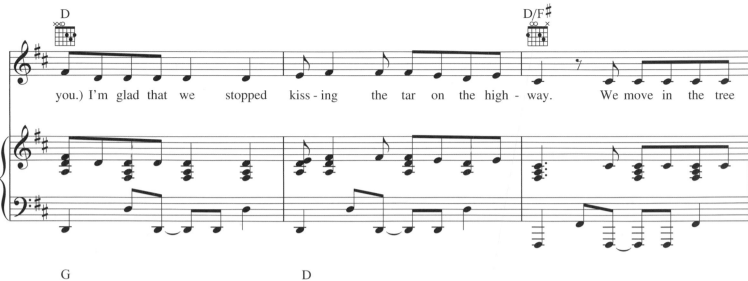

you.) I'm glad that we stopped kiss-ing the tar on the high-way. We move in the tree

streets, I'd like it if you stayed. And I like

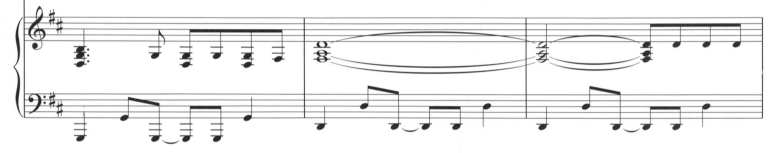

you. And I like you.

And I like you.

ROYALS

Words and Music by ELLA YELICH-O'CONNOR
and JOEL LITTLE

In a torn up town,
we're fine with this.
no post - code
We did - n't come from

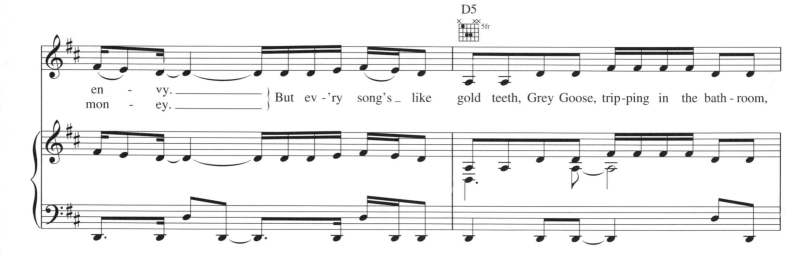

D5

en - vy. _____ } But ev -'ry song's _ like gold teeth, Grey Goose, trip-ping in the bath-room,
mon - ey. _____

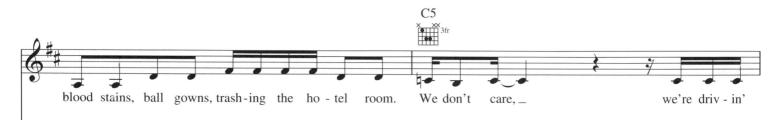

C5

blood stains, ball gowns, trash-ing the ho - tel room. We don't care, _ we're driv - in'

G5

D5

Cad - il -lacs in our dreams. _ But ev -'ry-bod-y's like Cris - tal, May-bach, dia-monds on your time-piece,

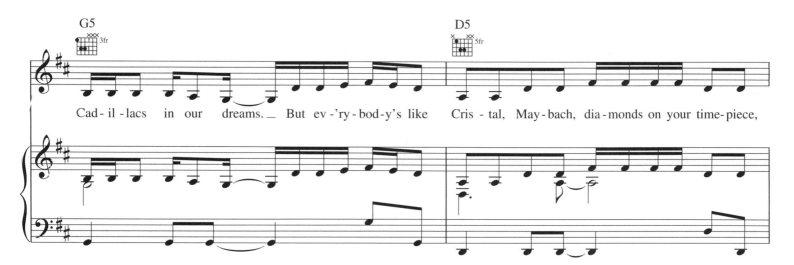

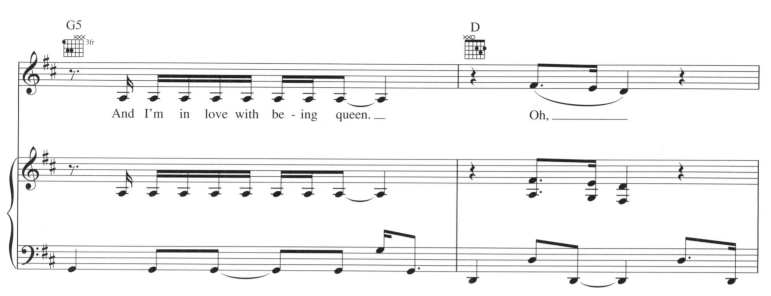

G5

D

And I'm in love with be-ing queen. ___ Oh, ___

C5

oh, ___ oh, ___ life is great with-out a care. ___ We aren't

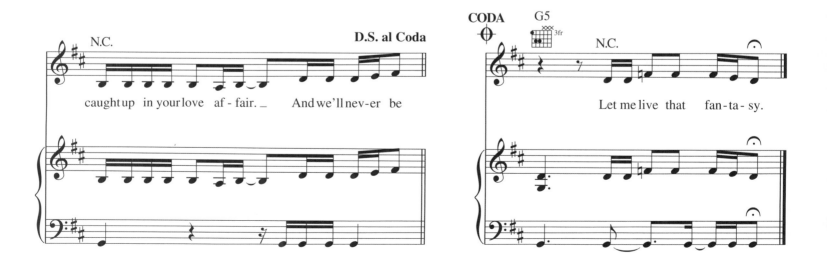

N.C.

D.S. al Coda

caught up in your love af-fair. ___ And we'll nev-er be

CODA G5

N.C.

Let me live that fan-ta-sy.

RIBS

Words and Music by ELLA YELICH-O'CONNOR
and JOEL LITTLE

With movement

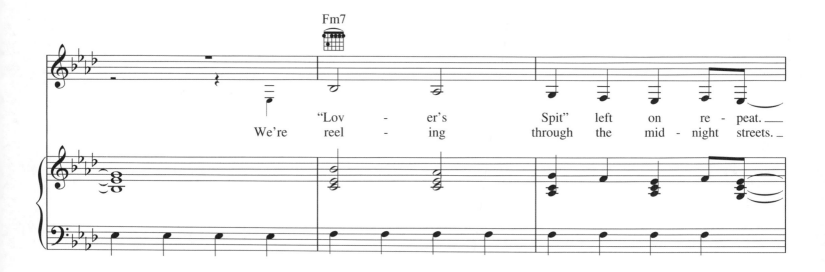

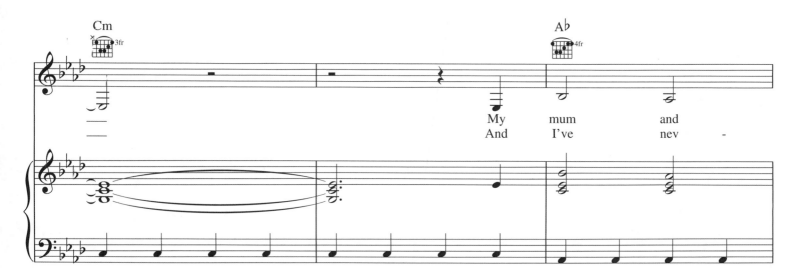

wish you would be all the time. ___ The

drink you spilt all o-ver me, ___ "Lov-er's Spit" ___ left on re-peat. ___ My
This dream is-n't feel-ing sweet, _ we're reel-ing through _ the moon-lit streets _ and

mum and dad ___ let me stay home, it drives you cra-zy, get-ting old. ___ The
I've nev-er ___ felt more a-lone, it feels so sca-ry get-ting old. ___ The

drink you spilt all o-ver me, ___ "Lov-er's Spit" ___ left on re-peat. ___ My
This dream is-n't feel-ing sweet, _ we're reel-ing through _ the moon-lit streets. _ And

mum and dad ___ let me stay home, it drives you cra - zy, get - ting old. ___
I've nev - er ___ felt more a - lone, it

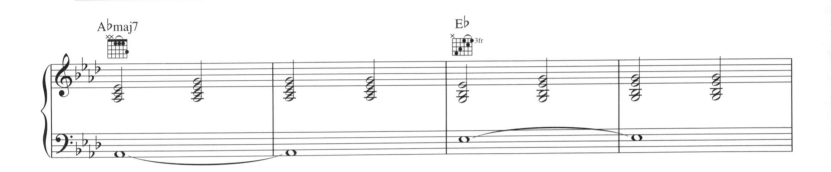

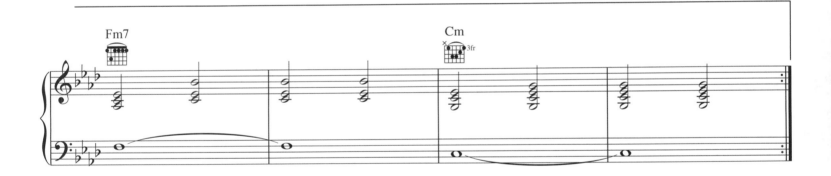

feels so scar - y get - ting old. ___

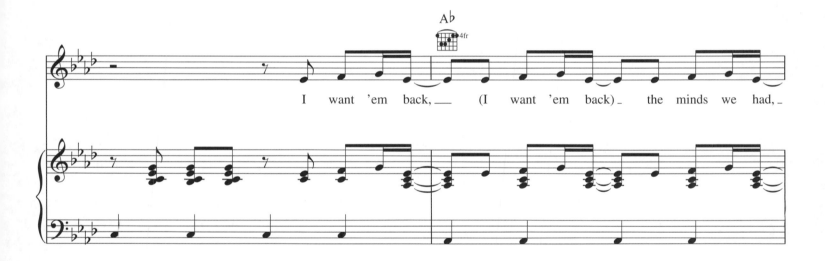

I want 'em back, __ (I want 'em back) _ the minds we had, _

__ (the minds we had). _ How all the thoughts (how all the thoughts) moved round our heads, _

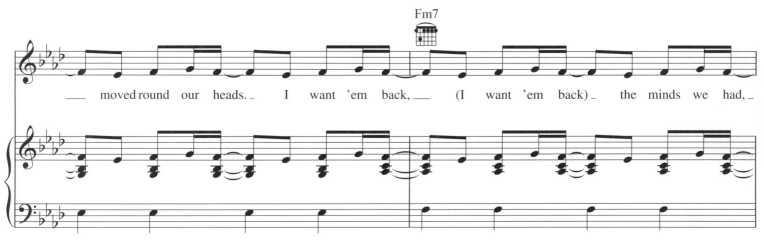

moved round our heads. I want 'em back, (I want 'em back) the minds we had,

(the minds we had). It's not e-nough, it's not e-nough to feel the lack,

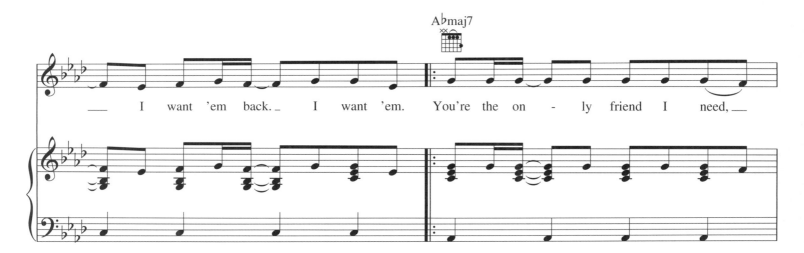

I want 'em back. I want 'em. You're the on-ly friend I need,

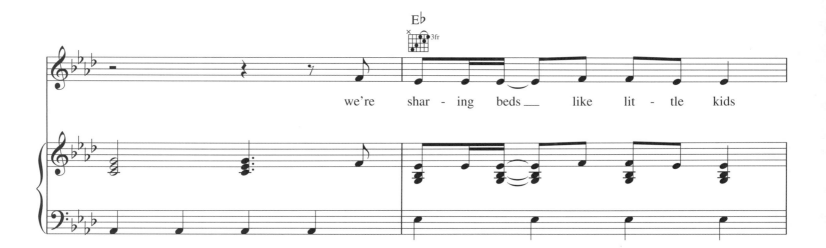

we're shar-ing beds like lit-tle kids

Repeat and Fade

Optional Ending

BUZZCUT SEASON

Words and Music by ELLA YELICH-O'CONNOR
and JOEL LITTLE

Ambient Electro Pop

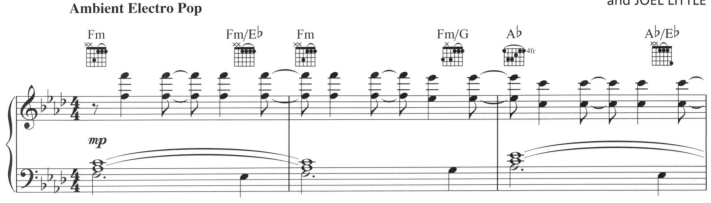

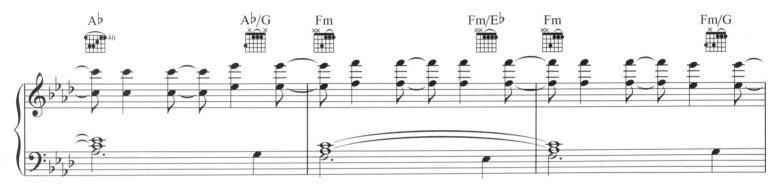

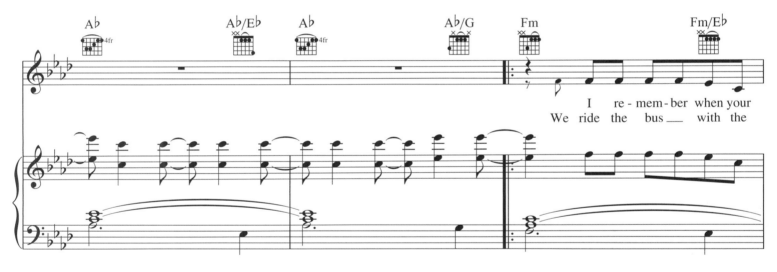

I re - mem - ber when your
We ride the bus ___ with the

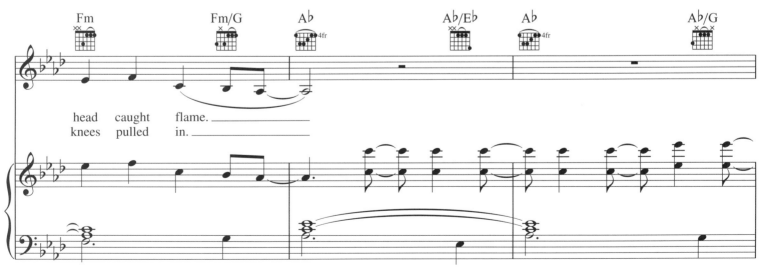

head caught flame. _____
knees pulled in. _____

D.S. al Coda
(take 3rd ending)

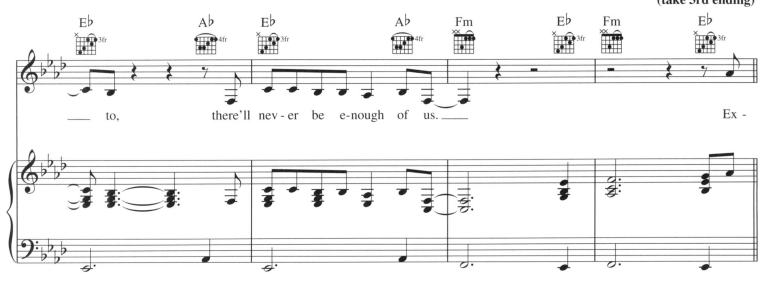

to, there'll nev-er be e-nough of us. Ex -

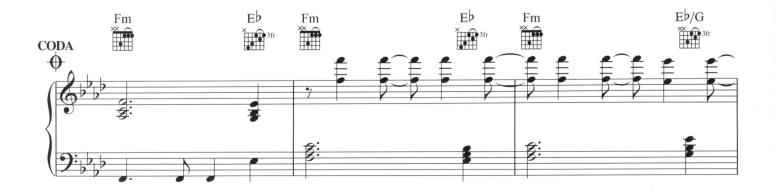

CODA

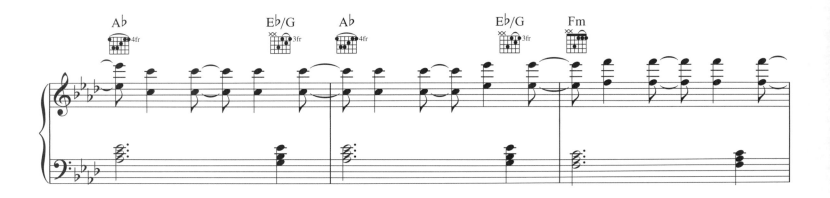

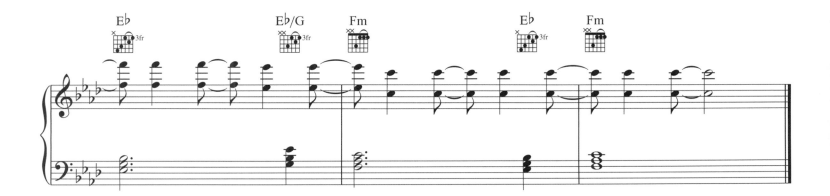

TEAM

Words and Music by ELLA YELICH-O'CONNOR
and JOEL LITTLE

Moderate Pop

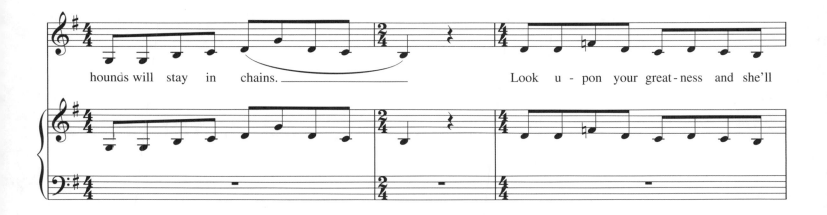

* Recorded a half-step lower

send the call out, send the call out, send the call out, send the call out, send the call out, send the call out,

send the call out, send the call out, send the call out, send the call out.

G

Call all the la - dies out, they're in their fi - ne - ry.

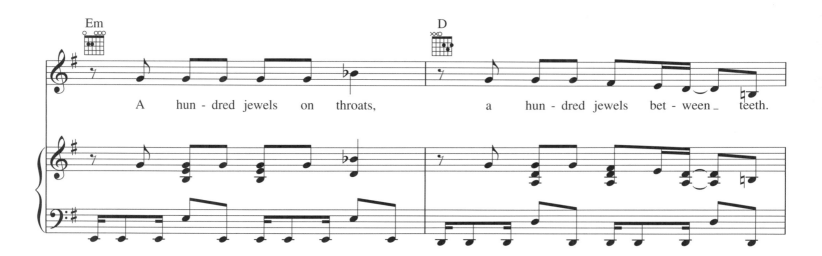

Em

A hun - dred jewels on throats,

D

a hun - dred jewels bet - ween_ teeth.

Now, bring my boys _____ in, _____ their skin in cra - ters like the moon. __

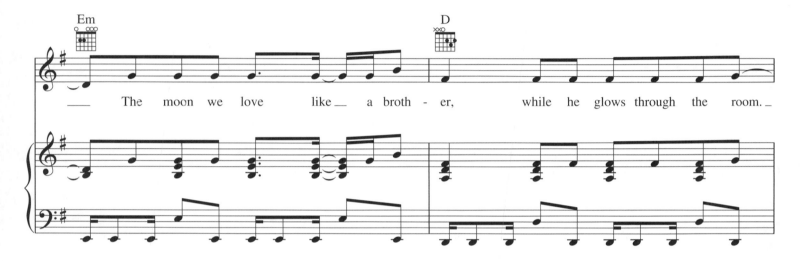

__ The moon we love like __ a broth - er, while he glows through the room. __

Danc - ing 'round the lies we tell. __ Danc - ing 'round big eyes as well, __ ah. _____

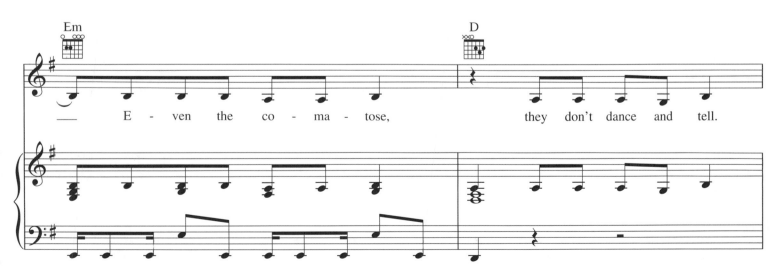

__ E - ven the co - ma - tose, they don't dance and tell.

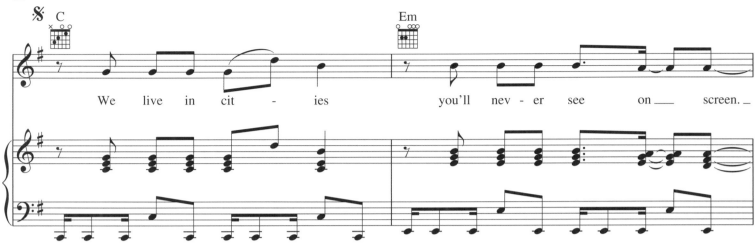

We live in cit - ies you'll nev-er see on ___ screen. ___

___ Not ve-ry pret - ty, but we sure know how to run things. ___

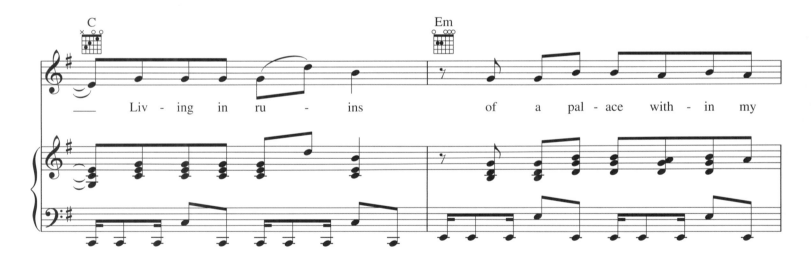

___ Liv - ing in ru - ins of a pal - ace with - in my

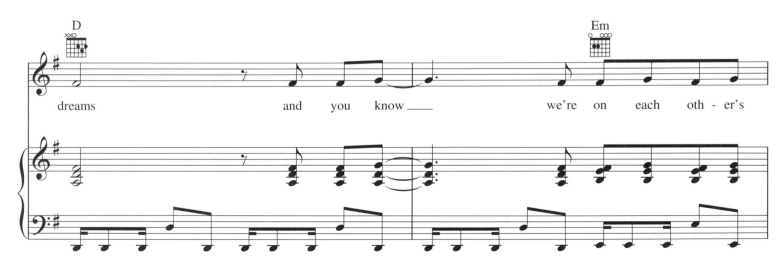

dreams and you know ___ we're on each oth - er's

team. I'm kind of o-ver get-ting told to throw my

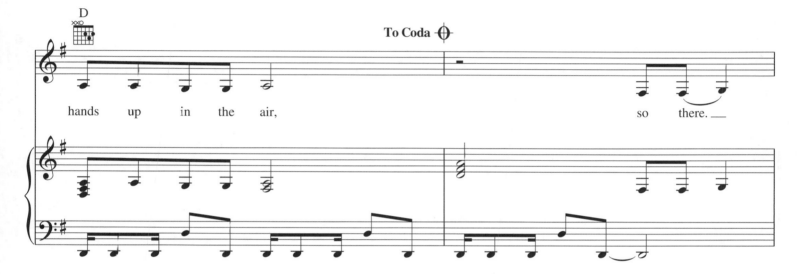

To Coda ⊕

hands up in the air, so there. ___

So all the cups got broke, shards be-neath our ___ feet, ___ but it was-n't my fault.

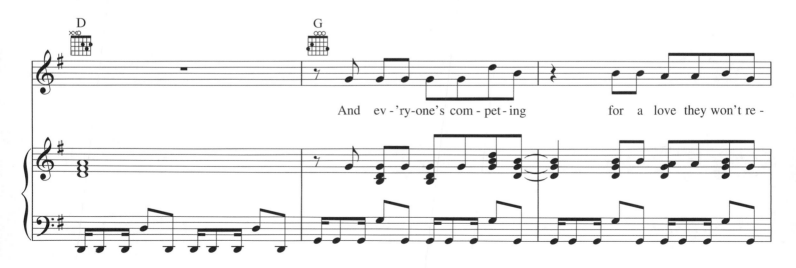

And ev-'ry-one's com-pet-ing for a love they won't re -

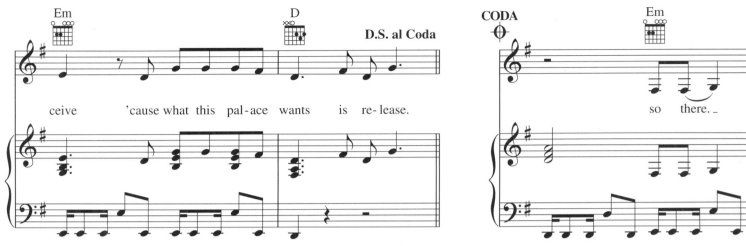

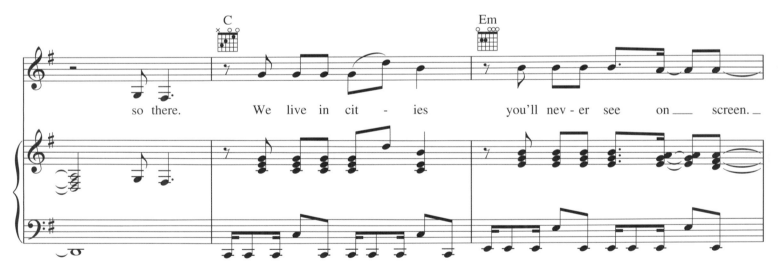

of the pa-lace with-in my dreams and you know ___ we're on each oth-er's

team. We're on each oth-er's team, and you know, ___

___ we're on each oth-er's team. We're on each oth-er's

team, and you know, ___ and you know, and you know. ___

GLORY AND GORE

Words and Music by ELLA YELICH-O'CONNOR
and JOEL LITTLE

Moderate Ballad

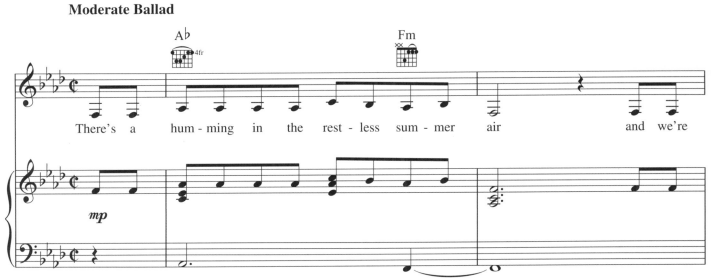

There's a hum-ming in the rest-less sum-mer air and we're

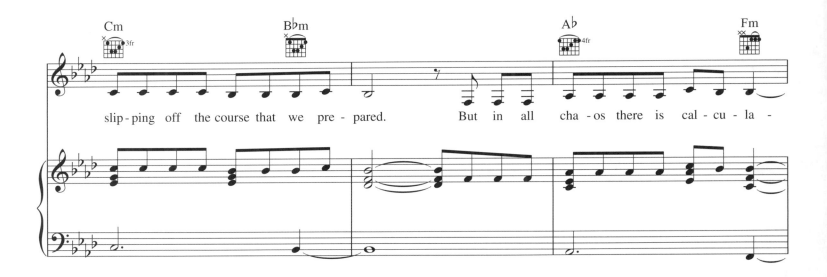

slip-ping off the course that we pre-pared. But in all cha-os there is cal-cu-la-

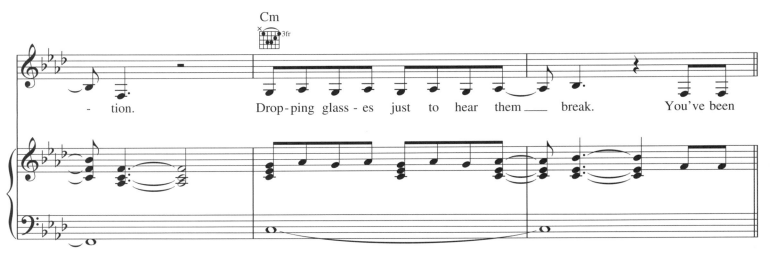

-tion. Drop-ping glass-es just to hear them ___ break. You've been

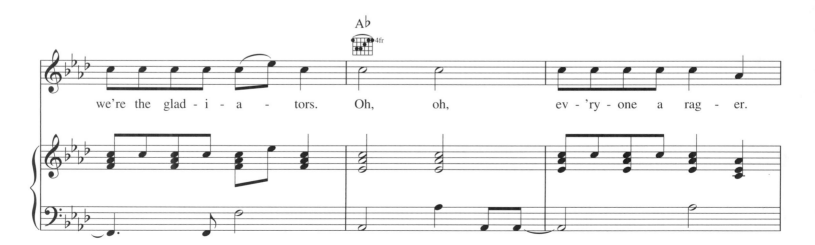

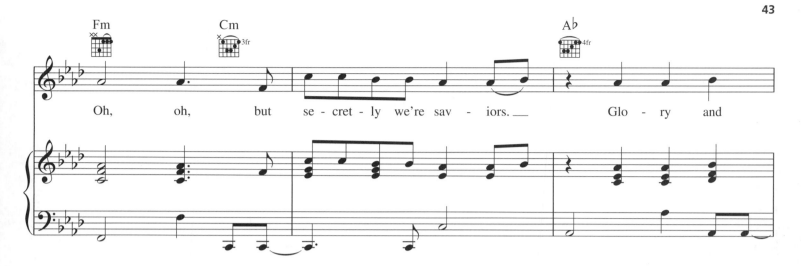

Oh, oh, but se - cret - ly we're sav - iors. __ Glo - ry and

gore go hand in hand, that's why we're mak - ing head - lines.

To Coda ⊕

Oh, oh, you could try and take us. Oh, oh, but

victo - ry's con - ta - gious. __

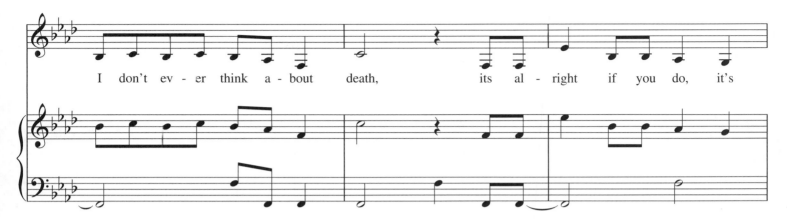

I don't ev - er think a - bout death, its al - right if you do, it's

fine. We glad - i - ate, but I

guess we're real - ly fight - ing our - selves.

Rough - ing up our minds so we're read - y when the kill time comes.

Wide a - wake in bed, words in my brain.

Sec - ret - ly you love this, do you e - ven want to go free?

N.C.

D.S. al Coda

Let me in the ring, I'll show you what that big word means.

CODA

Fm   Cm

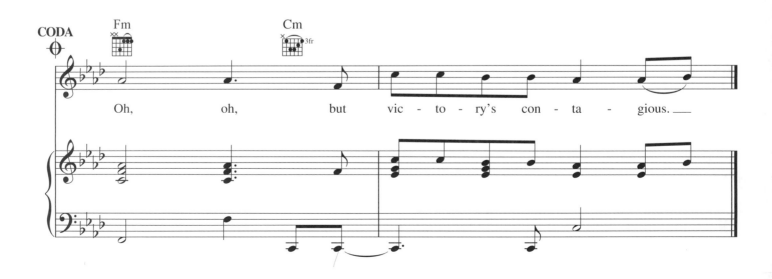

Oh, oh, but vic - to - ry's con - ta - gious. ___

STILL SANE

Words and Music by ELLA YELICH-O'CONNOR
and JOEL LITTLE

Ambient Ballad

To-day is my birth-day and I'm rid-ing high.

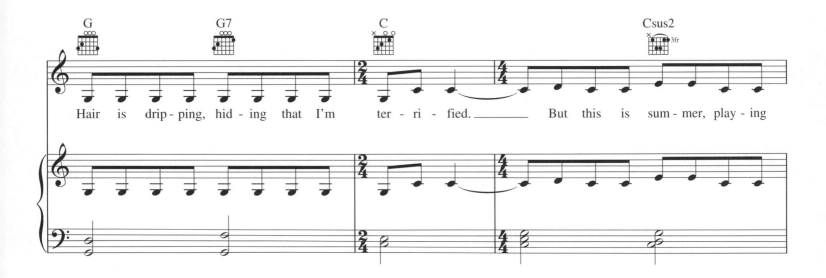

Hair is drip-ping, hid-ing that I'm ter-ri-fied. But this is sum-mer, play-ing

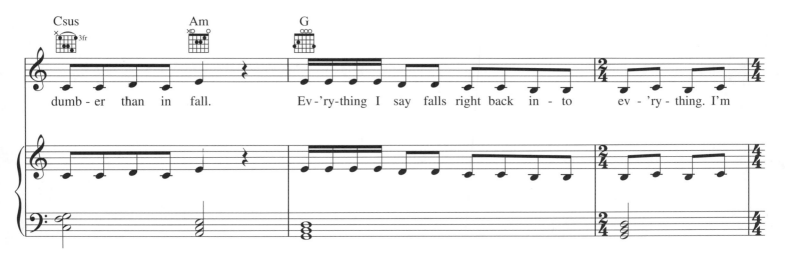

dumb-er than in fall. Ev-'ry-thing I say falls right back in-to ev-'ry-thing. I'm

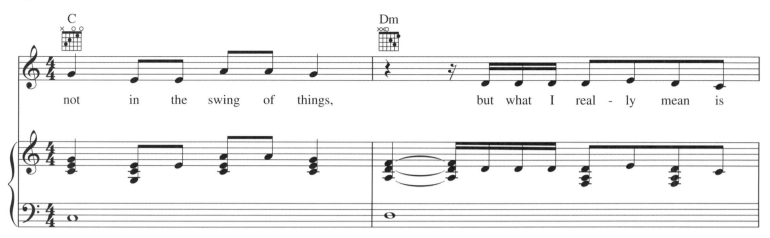

not in the swing of things, but what I real - ly mean is

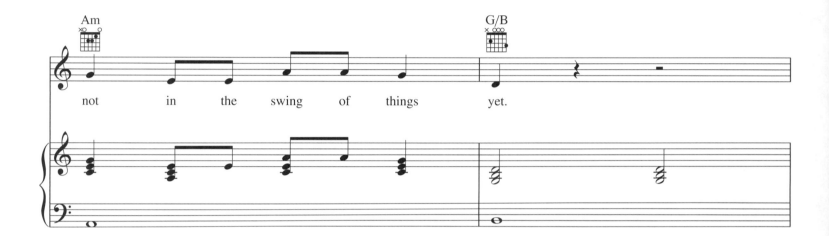

not in the swing of things yet.

Rid-ing a-round_ on the bikes,_ we're still sane, I won't be her,_ trip-ping o - ver on-stage. Hey,_

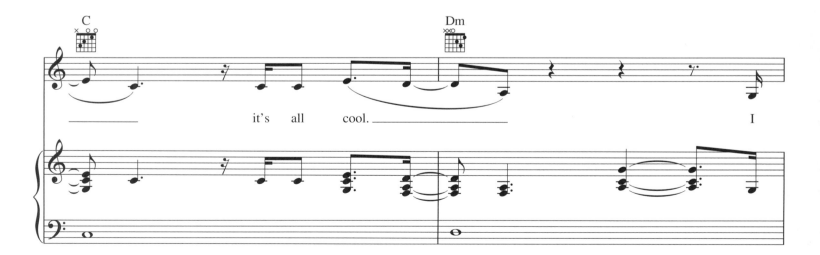

it's all cool._ I

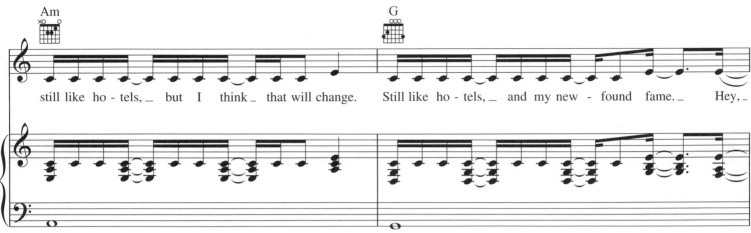

still like ho - tels, _ but I think _ that will change. Still like ho - tels, _ and my new - found fame. _ Hey, _

pro - mise I can stay _____ good.

Ev - 'ry - thing feels I'm lit - tle, but I'm com - ing for the

crown,
right.
I'm lit - tle, but I'm com - ing for you. _

50

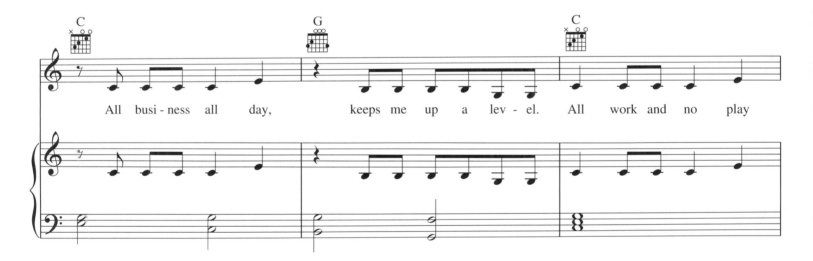

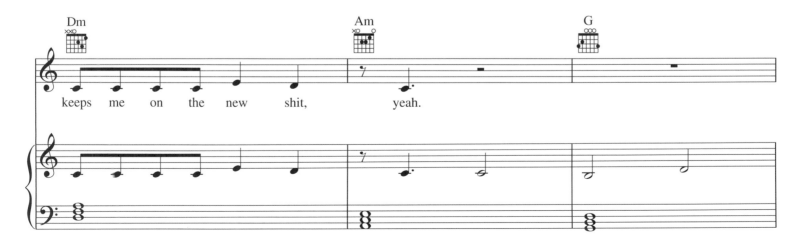

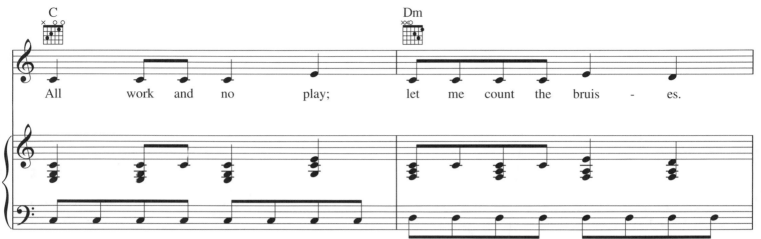

All work and no play; let me count the bruis - es.

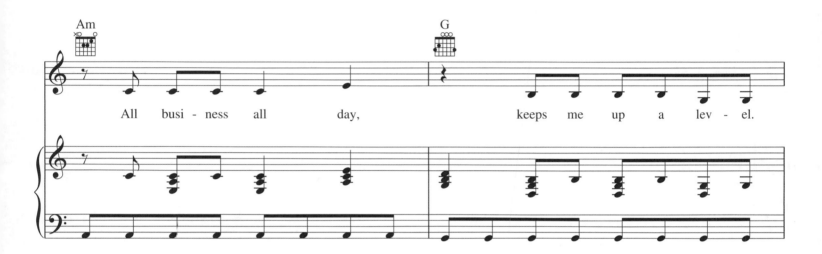

All busi - ness all day, keeps me up a lev - el.

All work and no play; lone - ly on that new shit,

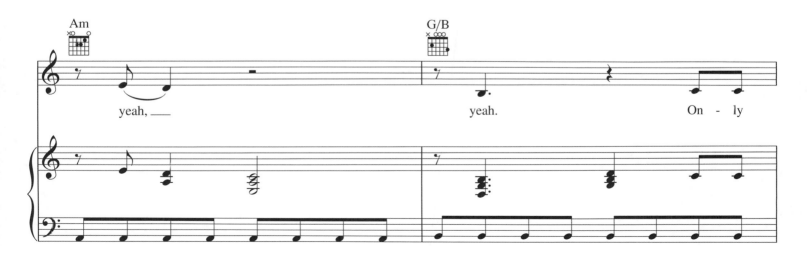

yeah, ___ yeah. On - ly

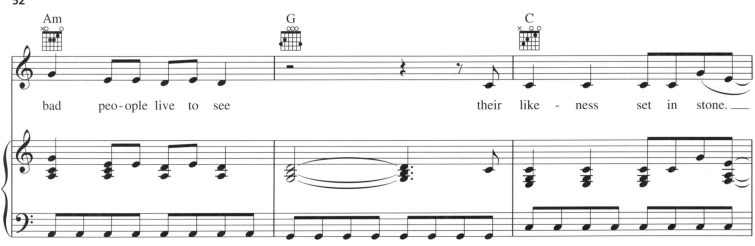

bad peo-ople live to see their like - ness set in stone. ___

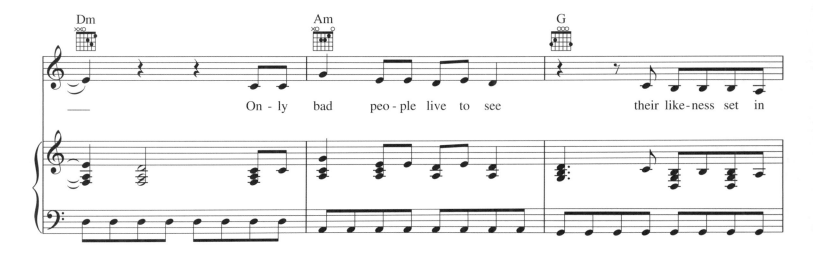

___ On - ly bad peo - ple live to see their like-ness set in

stone. I'm not in the swing of things,
What does that make me?

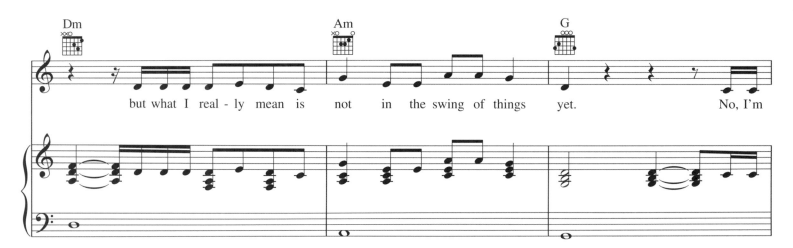

but what I real - ly mean is not in the swing of things yet. No, I'm

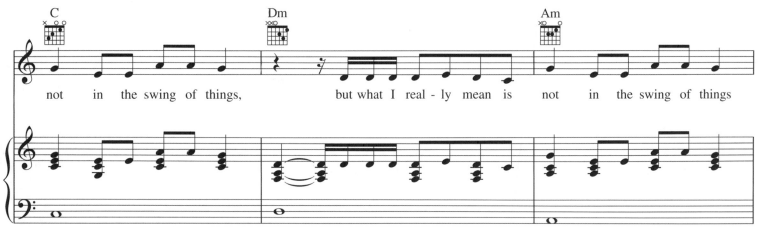

not in the swing of things, but what I real - ly mean is not in the swing of things

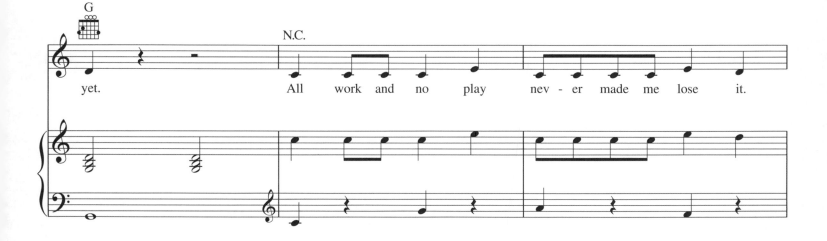

yet. All work and no play nev - er made me lose it.

All busi - ness all day, keeps me up a lev - el. All work and no play

keeps me on the new shit, yeah.

WHITE TEETH TEENS

Words and Music by ELLA YELICH-O'CONNOR
and JOEL LITTLE

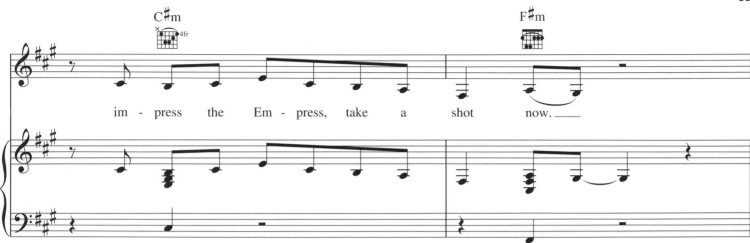

im - press the Em - press, take a shot now. ____

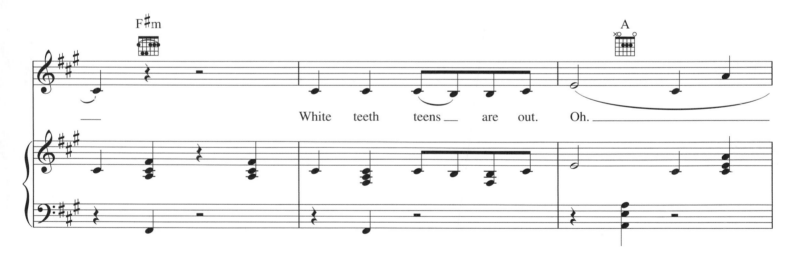

We've got the glow ____ in our mouths. ____

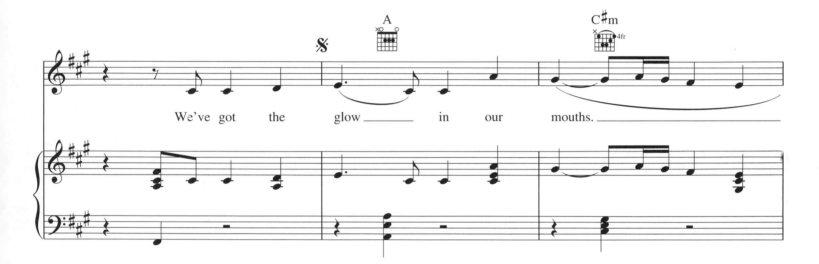

____ White teeth teens ____ are out. Oh. ____

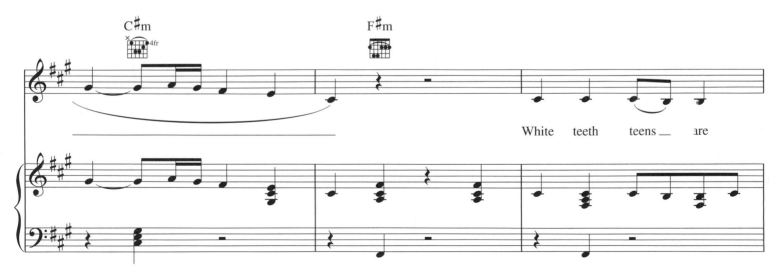

____ White teeth teens ____ are

up for it.   I know you love it when the hair - pins start to drop. __

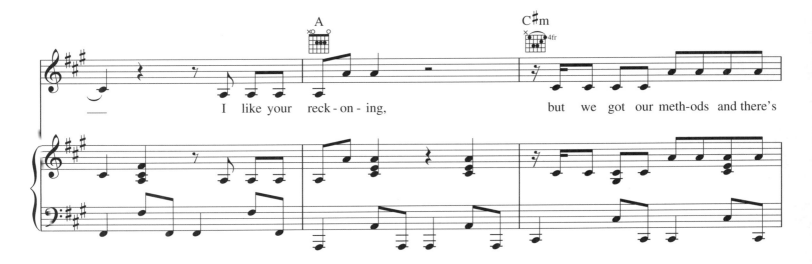

__   I like your reck - on - ing,   but we got our meth-ods and there's

noth - ing here to stop, ___ to stop this.

If you want, we'll help to - night to split its

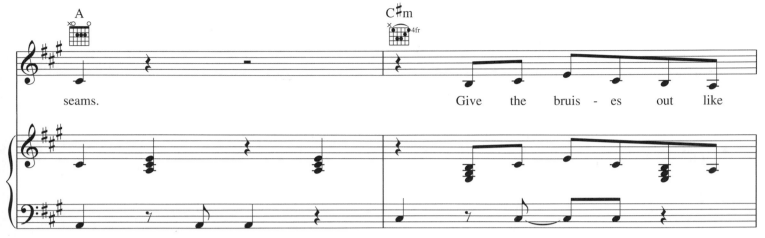

seams.   Give the bruis - es out like

gifts.   You'll get the pic - ture of your

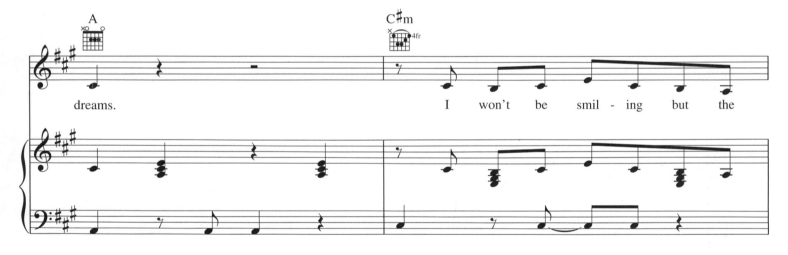

dreams.   I won't be smil - ing but the

D.S. al Coda

notes from my ad - mi - rers fill my dash - board just the same.
We've got the

58

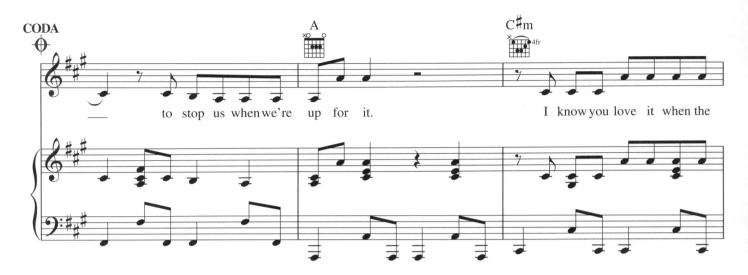

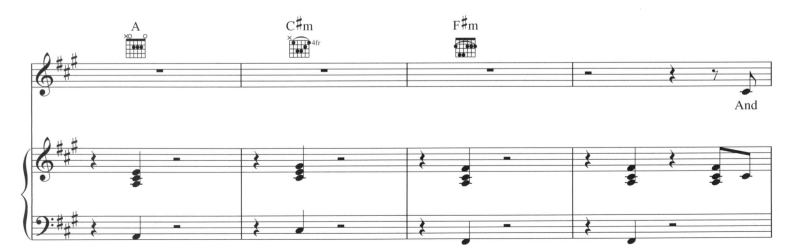

ev - 'ry - thing works out so good, I wear the robe like

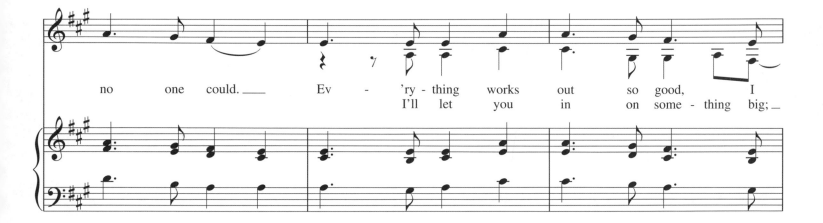

no one could. ___ Ev - 'ry - thing works out so good, I
I'll let you in on some - thing big; ___

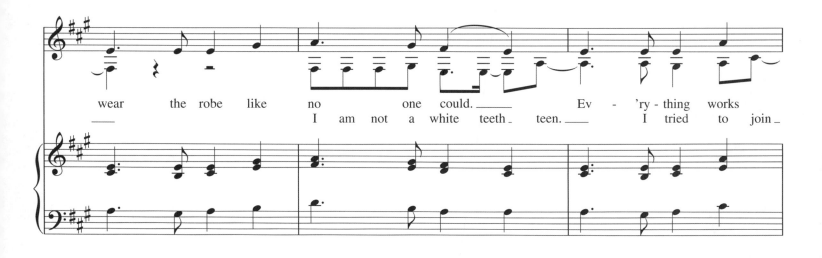

wear the robe like no one could. ___ Ev - 'ry - thing works
___ I am not a white teeth teen. ___ I tried to join ___

out so good, I wear the robe like no one could. ___
___ but nev - er did. ___ The way they are, the way they seem ___

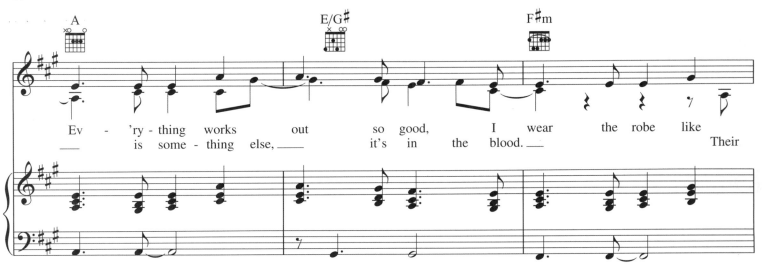

Ev - 'ry - thing works out so good, I wear the robe like
is some - thing else, __ it's in the blood. __ Their

no one could. __ Ev - 'ry - thing works out so good, I
mo - lars blink-ing like the lights __ in the un - der - pass __ where we all sit __

wear the robe like no one could. __ Ev - 'ry - thing works
__ and do noth-ing and love it.

out so good, I wear the robe like no one could. __

Ev - 'ry - thing works out so good, I wear the robe like

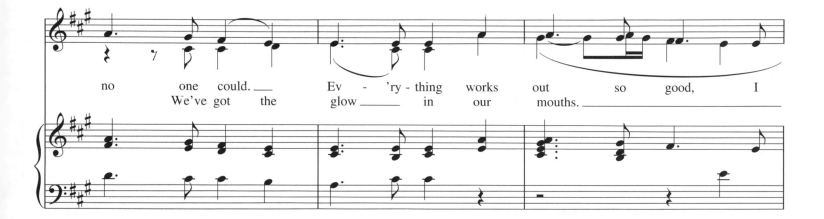

no one could. ___ Ev - 'ry - thing works out so good, I
We've got the glow ___ in our mouths. ___

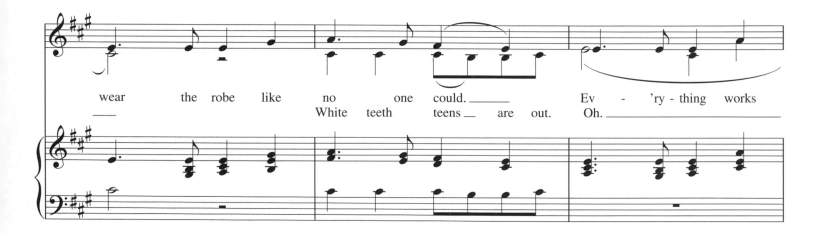

wear the robe like no one could. ___ Ev - 'ry - thing works
White teeth teens ___ are out. Oh. ___

out so good, I wear the robe like no one could. ___
White teeth teens ___ are out.

A WORLD ALONE

Words and Music by ELLA YELICH-O'CONNOR
and JOEL LITTLE

Ambient Electro-Pop

That slow burn wait ____ while it gets dark. ____

Bruis-ing the sun. ____ I feel grown up ____ with you ____ in your car, ____

I know it's dumb. ____
Ooh. ____

We've both got a mil-lion bad hab-its to kick, __ not sleep-ing is one. __ We're bit-ing our nails, __

Raise a glass, 'cause I'm not done say-ing it, they all want to get

rough, get a-way with it. Let 'em talk 'cause we're danc - ing in this world a - lone,

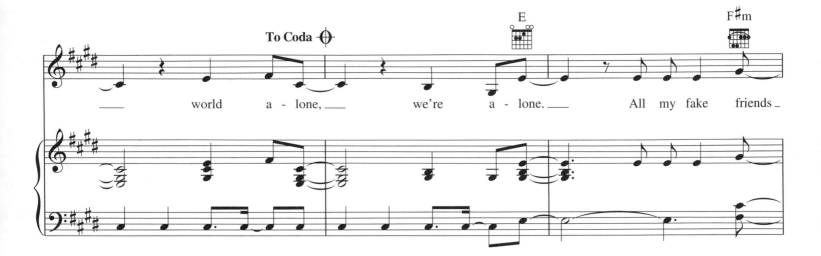

To Coda ⊕

___ world a - lone, ___ we're a - lone. ___ All my fake friends ___

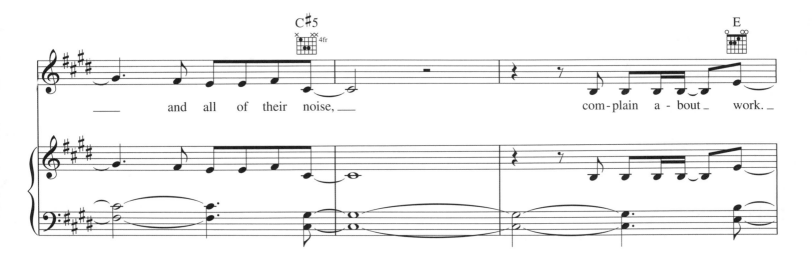

___ and all of their noise, ___ com-plain a-bout ___ work. ___

They're stud-y-ing busi-ness, I stud-ied the floor. And

you have-n't stopped smok-ing all _____ night. May-be the in-ter-net raised us, _____

or may-be peo-ple are jerks. _____ The peo-ple are talk-ing,

But not you. _____
peo-ple are talk-ing. The peo-ple are talk-ing, peo-ple are talk-ing.

D.S. al Coda

CODA

we're a - lone. ___ All the dou-ble-edged peo-ple and schemes, ___

they make a mess then go home and get clean. ___ You're my best friend and we're danc-

- ing in the world a - lone, ___ world a - lone, ___ we're all a - lone. ___

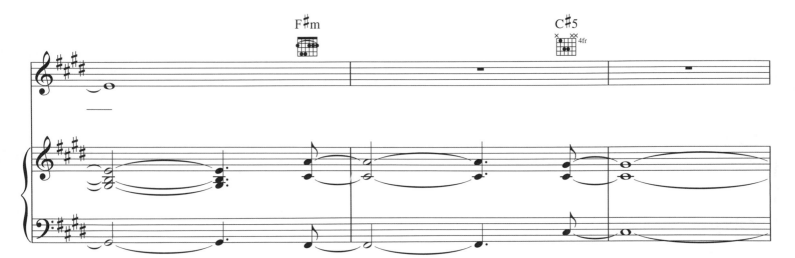

I know we're not _____

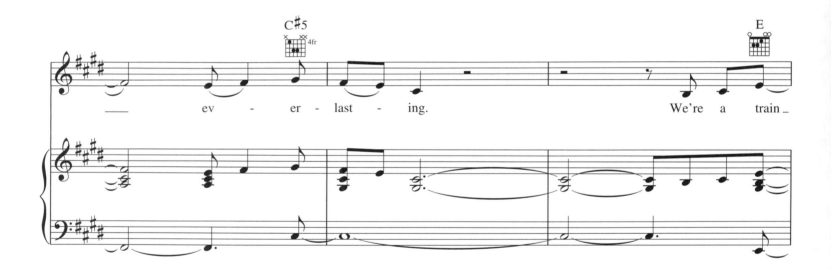

_____ ev - er - last - ing. We're a train _

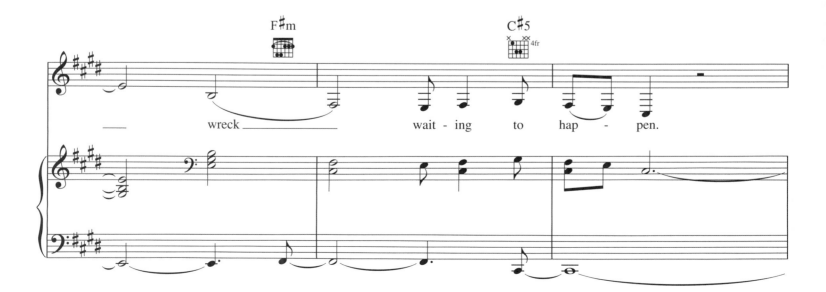

_____ wreck _____ wait - ing to hap - pen.

not done say-ing it, they all want to get rough, get a-way with it.

Let 'em talk 'cause we're danc - ing in this world a - lone, ___ world a - lone, ___

___ we're a - lone. ___ All the dou-ble-edged peo - ple and schemes, ___

they make a mess then go home and get clean. ___ You're my best friend and we're danc-

-ing in the world a - lone, __ world a - lone, __ we're all a - lone. __

__ The peo - ple are talk - ing, peo - ple are talk - ing. The peo - ple are talk - ing,

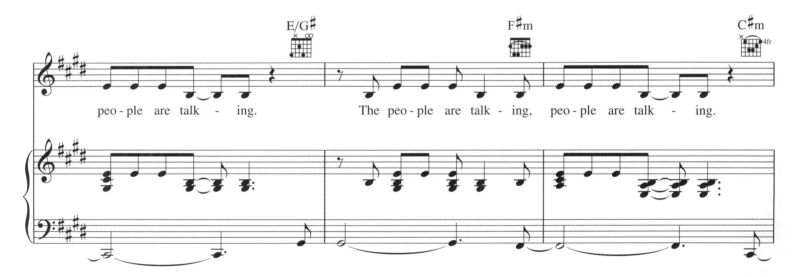

peo - ple are talk - ing. The peo - ple are talk - ing, peo - ple are talk - ing.

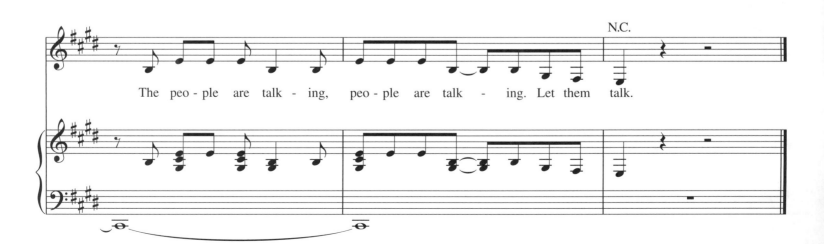

The peo - ple are talk - ing, peo - ple are talk - ing. Let them talk.